It's My State! ★ ★ ★ ★ ★

FLORIDA
The Sunshine State

Debra Hess and Lori Wiesenfeld

Cavendish
Square

New York

Published in 2015 by Cavendish Square Publishing, LLC
243 5th Avenue, Suite 136, New York, NY 10016

CPSIA Compliance Information: Batch #WS14CSQ

All websites were available and accurate when this book was sent to press.

Library of Congress Cataloging-in-Publication Data
Hess, Debra.
 Florida / Debra Hess and Lori Wiesenfeld. — Third edition.
    pages cm. — (It's my state!)
 Includes index.
 ISBN 978-1-62712-736-3 (hardcover) ISBN 978-1-62712-739-4 (ebook)
 1. Florida—Juvenile literature. I. Wiesenfeld, Lori P. II. Title.
 F311.3.H47 2014
 975.9—dc23
 2014004015

Editorial Director: Dean Miller
Editor, Third Edition: Nicole Sothard
Art Director: Jeffrey Talbot
Series Designer, Third Edition: Jeffrey Talbot
Layout Design, Third Edition: Erica Clendening
Production Manager: Jennifer Ryder-Talbot

Printed in the United States of America

FLORIDA ★ ★ ★ ★ ★
CONTENTS

State Tree: Sabal Palm

The majestic sabal palm, also known as sabal palmetto and cabbage palm, grows in almost any soil throughout the state of Florida. This towering tree, used for landscaping, food, and medicine, became the state tree in 1953.

State Bird: Mockingbird

Mockingbirds are usually about 10 inches (25 cm) long with wingspans of 15 inches (38 cm). They have grayish upper bodies, white undersides, and white patches on their tails and wings. This songbird frequently sings all night long and is a great mimic of other birds. The mockingbird became the state bird in 1927.

State Flower: Orange Blossom

Millions of these sweet-smelling white flowers bloom in central and south Florida. These flowers grow on the same tree that bears the famous Florida orange. The orange blossom was named the state flower in 1909.

FLORIDA

State Animal: Florida Panther

This pale-brown long-tailed cat hunts white-tailed deer and other smaller animals. Since the 1700s and 1800s, many feared this cat would attack humans and farm animals. As a result, people hunted the panthers until very few remained. Destruction of the cats' natural habitat has also been a problem. The Florida panther, on the endangered species list since 1967, became the state animal in 1982.

State Reptile: American Alligator

These cold-blooded creatures like to bask in the sun on logs or riverbanks. But they move amazingly quickly over short distances. The alligator has powerful jaws and can use its swinging tail as a weapon. Fortunately, it is no longer on the endangered species list. It became the state reptile in 1987.

State Beverage: Orange Juice

Have you ever had a glass of the juice of the species *Citrus sinensis* and its hybrids? Sure you have: it is orange juice! In 1967, it became Florida's official state beverage.

Ocean Drive, in Miami, is known for its architecture, beaches, and nightlife.

The Sunshine State

More than 89 million people travel to Florida every year for its sunny beaches, refreshing water, and other attractions. But Florida is so much more than a dream vacation spot. North of the beaches lie rolling hills and lush forests, while in the south a sprawling national park is home to hundreds of different endangered plants and animals.

Landscape and Regions

Florida is the southernmost state in the continental United States (Hawaii is farther south). The largest part of Florida is a peninsula that projects about 400 miles (640 km) into the sea. A peninsula is land that is surrounded by water on three sides. The northern part of Florida runs along the shore of the Gulf of Mexico. It is called the panhandle because it is shaped like the handle of a frying pan. The southern tip of the state is less than 100 miles (160 km) from Cuba.

Florida's current size and shape are a result of millions of years of geological change. Large pieces of rock, called plates, lie beneath Earth's surface. Over time these plates move around, combining and breaking landmasses, and shaping the features of Earth's surface. Erosion—the process of being worn away by wind, rain, and water current—changed

The Everglades is a region of tropical wetlands in the southern portion of Florida.

Florida's shape and landscape. Dirt, sand, shells, and rocks brought by the wind and ocean currents also shaped parts of Florida. Over time, sea creatures such as coral and mollusks lived and died on the coasts of Florida. Their remains hardened into rocks and minerals and added mass to Florida's coasts.

One million years ago, Earth's climate turned much colder. Large amounts of ocean water turned into ice, and large masses of ice called glaciers covered much of the planet. As a result, the water level in the oceans sank, and at that time, the land that is now Florida was twice its current size. When this Ice Age ended, water levels rose, and much of that land was covered. The rise in water levels also formed swamps.

The Florida peninsula lies on the relatively flat land formation called the Florida Platform. The highest point in the entire state—only 345 feet (105 m) high—is Britton Hill, in the north. Florida has 53,927 square miles (139,670 sq km) of land, making it the twenty-sixth-largest state in the country.

The area of Florida known as the Coastal Lowlands stretches around the coastal borders of the state. The lowlands are covered with forests of sabal palm and cypress. The best-known area of the Coastal Lowlands is the Everglades. The Everglades cover a large

This view from space shows Florida, the Gulf of Mexico to the west, and the Atlantic Ocean to the east.

FLORIDA
COUNTY MAP

ESCAMBIA
SANTA ROSA
OKA-LOOSA
WALTON
HOLMES
WASHINGTON
JACKSON
CAL-HOUN
BAY
GADSDEN
LEON
LIBERTY
WAKULLA
GULF
FRANKLIN
JEFFERSON
MADISON
HAMILTON
TAYLOR
SUWANNEE
LAFAYETTE
COLUMBIA
BAKER
NASSAU
DUVAL
UNION
CLAY
ST. JOHNS
GIL-CHRIST
BRADFORD
ALACHUA
PUTNAM
FLAGLER
DIXIE
LEVY
MARION
VOLUSIA
CITRUS
SUMTER
LAKE
SEMINOLE
ORANGE
HERNANDO
PASCO
OSCEOLA
BREVARD
PINELLAS
HILLS-BOROUGH
POLK
INDIAN RIVER
OKEE-CHOBEE
ST. LUCIE
MANATEE
HARDEE
HIGH-LANDS
MARTIN
SARASOTA
DESOTO
CHARLOTTE
GLADES
PALM BEACH
LEE
HENDRY
COLLIER
BROWARD
MIAMI-DADE
MONROE

FLORIDA
POPULATION BY COUNTY

County	Population	County	Population	County	Population
Alachua County	247,336	Jackson County	49,746	Suwannee County	41,551
Baker County	27,115	Jefferson County	14,761	Taylor County	22,570
Bay County	168,852	Lafayette County	8,870	Union County	15,535
Bradford County	28,520	Lake County	297,052	Volusia County	494,593
Brevard County	543,376	Lee County	618,754	Wakulla County	30,776
Broward County	1,748,066	Leon County	275,487	Walton County	55,043
Calhoun County	14,625	Levy County	40,801	Washington County	24,896
Charlotte County	159,978	Liberty County	8,365		
Citrus County	141,236	Madison County	19,224		
Clay County	190,865	Manatee County	322,833		
Collier County	321,520	Marion County	331,298		
Columbia County	67,531	Martin County	146,318		
DeSoto County	34,862	Miami-Dade County	2,496,435		
Dixie County	16,422	Monroe County	73,090		
Duval County	864,263	Nassau County	73,314		
Escambia County	297,619	Okaloosa County	180,822		
Flagler County	95,696	Okeechobee County	39,996		
Franklin County	11,549	Orange County	1,145,956		
Gadsden County	46,389	Osceola County	268,685		
Gilchrist County	16,939	Palm Beach County	1,320,134		
Glades County	12,884	Pasco County	464,697		
Gulf County	15,863	Pinellas County	916,542		
Hamilton County	14,799	Polk County	602,095		
Hardee County	27,731	Putnam County	74,364		
Hendry County	39,140	St. Johns County	190,039		
Hernando County	172,778	St. Lucie County	277,789		
Highlands County	98,786	Santa Rosa County	151,372		
Hillsborough County	1,229,226	Sarasota County	379,448		
Holmes County	19,927	Seminole County	422,718		
Indian River County	138,028	Sumter County	93,420		

Source: U.S. Bureau of the Census, 2010

Miami-Dade County

Orange County

Lake Okeechobee is the seventh largest freshwater lake in the United States. It is more than half the size of Rhode Island.

portion of the state, stretching from Lake Okeechobee, the state's largest lake, to the Gulf of Mexico. Mangrove trees, ferns, and a razor-sharp plant called saw grass cover much of this marshy wetland. The wildlife in the park includes alligators, waterfowl, and hundreds of kinds of frogs, turtles, and snakes.

For many years, people considered the Everglades a worthless swamp. Developers began to drain the Everglades in order to use the land. They had dreams of building hotels and tourist resorts in this region. Wildlife was killed, and habitats were destroyed.

Since the 1930s, many nature enthusiasts, such as Ernest F. Coe, worked toward passing laws to protect the Everglades. In 1947, Marjory Stoneman Douglas wrote *The Everglades: River of Grass*, a book that called attention to the wonders of the Everglades, begging the world to preserve its sensitive **ecosystem**. Many plants and animals living there were endangered. Destroying their habitat would make them disappear forever. The efforts of the Everglades' supporters paid off in 1947 when President Harry Truman dedicated Everglades National Park, protecting a large portion of the region—and the wildlife within it— from **development**.

The southernmost parts of the state are called the Florida Keys. This chain of islands is 110 miles (177 km) long. It stretches from Biscayne Bay—located on the southeastern coast of Florida—southwest, toward the Gulf of Mexico.

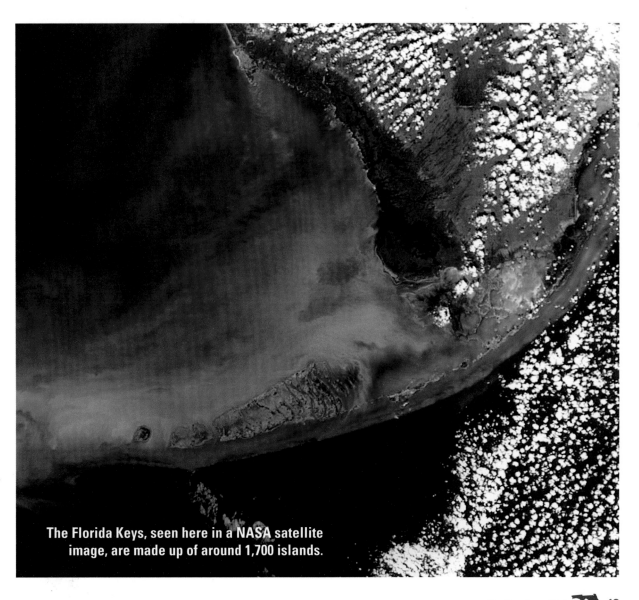

The Florida Keys, seen here in a NASA satellite image, are made up of around 1,700 islands.

★ 10 KEY SITES ★ ★ ★

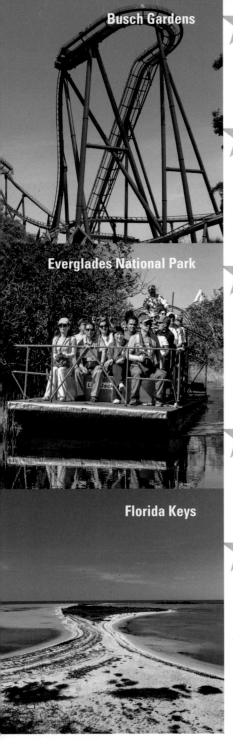

Busch Gardens

Everglades National Park

Florida Keys

1. Busch Gardens Tampa

This 335-acre (136 ha), African-themed park features rides and more than 2,700 animals. Visitors can see lions, gorillas, zebras, and even rhinos!

2. Castillo de San Marcos

Built in the late 1600s, Castillo de San Marcos in St. Augustine was originally built to defend Florida against pirates hunting Spanish ships in the area. The fort, which is one of the oldest in America, is made of shells.

3. Everglades National Park

The Everglades is an area of tropical wetlands at the southern tip of Florida. Everglades National Park protects around 20 percent of it. More than 9 million people go each year to explore the park and the wildlife, which includes alligators, manatees, and various birds.

4. Florida Keys

The Florida Keys are a group of islands off the southern coast of the state. Known for their warm, tropical weather, the Keys are a popular place to fish, dive, and snorkel.

5. Kennedy Space Center

The Kennedy Space Center, near Cape Canaveral, is the **launch** site for human space flights, including the Space Shuttle. The visitor center features exhibits, spacecraft, and tours. You can even experience a simulated, or pretend, space-shuttle launch!

FLORIDA ★ ★ ★ ★ ★

6. Miami Children's Museum

This museum is a place where children of all ages and their parents can learn and play. Kids can learn about animals, learn how to stay safe and healthy, make art, and play music.

7. Museum of Science and Industry

Tampa's Museum of Science and Industry, or MOSI, is dedicated to helping visitors understand science, industry, and technology. A butterfly garden, rope course, and a section on the human body are just some of the exhibits there.

8. Sanibel Island

This island off the southwestern coast of Florida is a popular place for families to spend their vacations. While there visitors can find seashells on the beach, explore the J.N. "Ding" Darling National Wildlife Refuge, and bike around the entire island.

9. SeaWorld Orlando

SeaWorld is a theme and zoological park that focuses on marine life. Attractions include rides and animal exhibits in which visitors can learn about and see different marine animals, including stingrays, sea turtles, and killer whales.

10. Walt Disney World

The most visited attraction in the world, Walt Disney World features four theme parks, two water parks, restaurants, and hotels. Located in Orlando, some of the parks you can visit include Magic Kingdom, Epcot, Hollywood Studios, and Animal Kingdom.

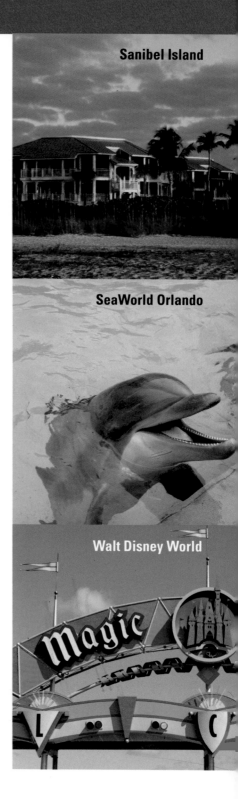

Sanibel Island

SeaWorld Orlando

Walt Disney World

Florida has more than 650 miles (1,062 km) of beaches, many of which attract tourists from all over the world.

The only living coral reef in the United States is here. Some of the islands also have tropical forests. But many people live on the islands in close-knit communities. Bridges and the Overseas Highway connect most of the islands. But some islands can be reached only by boat. Key West, on the western end of the islands, is the southernmost city in the continental United States.

Florida's highest points rise from the sea with hilly pine forests in the northwestern corner of the state. The Western Highlands are low compared to many other parts of the United States. Rolling hills and small villages surround the highlands.

East of the Western Highlands and north of the Coastal Lowlands are the Marianna Lowlands. Hills and valleys make up this section of Florida, where many people still farm. The Tallahassee Hills lie farther east. Oak and pine trees cover the hills, which slope toward the famous Suwannee River to the east. The Suwannee River flows south from the Okefenokee Swamp in Georgia, down through parts of Florida, and into the Gulf of Mexico. In the center of the Florida peninsula is a 250-mile (400-km) stretch of land known as the Central Highlands. Flat grassy plains, citrus groves, and lakeside communities make up this area.

Climate

Florida's climate is hot and humid. Heavy rains fall from April to November. As one native Floridian said of the rain and humidity, "We may not have to deal with cold and snow, but Florida is a bad hair state."

The state has the longest coastline of any U.S. state except Alaska. When temperatures soar, there are plenty of coastal places to swim and cool off.

Floridians may not have to deal with freezing temperatures and snowstorms, but from the beginning of June to the end of November, they have to worry about hurricanes. A hurricane is a tropical storm with wind speeds of at least 74 miles per hour (119 kph). A hurricane begins over an ocean, where the sun warms the surface of the water and causes the water to **evaporate**. The evaporated water floats into the air and forms thunderclouds. The rotation of Earth sends these storm clouds spinning toward land. When a hurricane hits a developed area, the flooding can destroy buildings and kill people.

More hurricanes strike Florida than any other state. The damage can be massive. In 1992, Hurricane Andrew caused 65 deaths and destruction that totaled $25 billion. Floridians worked together with people from other parts of the country to repair and rebuild their communities.

Winds from a hurricane blow palm trees in Miami.

Wildlife

More than 90 species of mammals live in different parts of the state, including the black bear, puma, gray fox, and otter. More types of fish and shellfish are found in Florida's waters than in any other part of the world. The coastal waters are filled with shrimp, oysters, crabs, scallops, clams, conchs, and crayfish. Bass and catfish swim in the freshwater lakes and rivers. The oceans are full of grouper, mackerel, marlin, and trout. More than one thousand species of fish have been identified in Florida's waters.

Fish are not the only animals you will find in the water. Bottlenose dolphins inhabit Florida's coastal waters. But swimming with or feeding dolphins can be dangerous for both humans and animals. When traveling through the swamp, animals—including humans—must look out for alligators lurking in the waters.

Five hundred species of wild birds soar over Florida's waters and land. These include quail, cuckoos, ospreys, pelicans, woodpeckers, robins, pigeons, storks, and bald eagles. On the water you might see herons, ducks, ibis, egrets, or flamingos. Wild turkeys also roam across some of Florida's woodlands and open forests. Human activity and the resulting changes to the **environment** almost completely killed off some of these birds. The bald eagle, a well-known symbol of the United States, **thrives** in the state, under a careful state management plan, after being removed from the federal threatened species list in 1997. (If an animal or plant is threatened, that means it is likely to become endangered.) The flamingo, heron, egret, and ibis almost became extinct in the 1800s after hunters killed them for their feathers, which were sold to hatmakers. Today, places such as Everglades National Park protect these beautiful birds.

The wood stork and Florida manatee are examples of the state's endangered animals. Endangered animals once had large populations, but now only very few remain. Their numbers decreased when hunters killed them for skins, feathers, or food. Car accidents (or collisions with boats in the case of the manatee) and habitat destruction also reduced their populations. The federal government stepped in and listed these animals as endangered species.

Once an animal is listed as endangered, it is illegal to hunt that animal or harm it in any way. Some endangered animals are taken to protected places. Sometimes humans try to recreate the animals' natural habitat to help them live longer and breed. The Everglades is home to many endangered animals. Through the efforts of Floridians and nature lovers across the country, many endangered animals and plants have had a chance to increase their numbers and survive.

Flamingos can sometimes be found in the marshy wetlands of the Everglades or in the waters along the Keys.

American Alligator

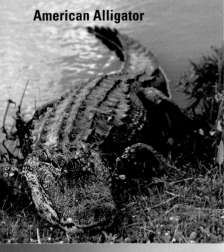

Cypress

Florida Manatee

1. State Reptile: American Alligator

The American Alligator lives in the wetlands and swamps of Florida. Males grow to be 10 to 15 feet (3 to 4.6 m) long, and they can weigh 1,000 pounds (453 kg). Females grow to be about 9.8 feet (3 m) long.

2. Bottlenose Dolphin

Bottlenose dolphins track their prey through echolocation. They make clicking sounds, which travel underwater until they reach an object, and then the sounds bounce back, revealing the object's location, shape, and size.

3. Cypress

The bald cypress, which grows into a giant tree, is normally found by lakes, in swamps, and along streams. The pond cypress tree, a much smaller variety, grows in ponds with still or slow-moving water. It is native to the Everglades.

4. State Mammal: Florida Manatee

The manatee is a large, gentle mammal that lives in Florida's warm waters. Each year, many manatees are injured or killed by boats when they get tangled in fishing lines. Land development has also decreased the manatees' natural habitat. The Florida manatee is an endangered species.

5. State Animal: Florida Panther

An endangered species, there are only an estimated 100 to 160 adult Florida panthers living in Southern Florida. Males are around 7 feet (2 m) long while females are around 6 feet (1.8 m) long. Males weigh about 130 pounds (59 kg) and females weigh 70 to 75 (32 to 34 kg) pounds.

6. Mangrove

These medium-sized tropical trees are found along the coast of Florida and the Florida Keys, generally in swampy areas. Mangroves' tangled roots provide shelter to various fish and crustaceans.

7. State Flower: Orange Blossom

The state flower is often used to make perfume because of its strong, sweet fragrance. After the flowers bloom, orange fruit starts to grow. These oranges are called navel oranges.

8. State Tree: Sabal Palm

The state tree can grow up to 66 feet (20 m) high. It is featured on Florida's state seal and the state quarter. Part of the sabal palm's frond, called the heart, is sometimes used as food. The heart is the main ingredient in a heart of palm salad.

9. Sea Turtles

Five types of sea turtles live in Florida's waters. Green, hawksbill, Kemp's ridley, and loggerhead turtles are endangered, and the leatherback is threatened, or likely to become endangered.

10. Southern Magnolia

The southern magnolia, also known as the evergreen magnolia, grows anywhere from 60 to 90 feet (18-28 m) in height. The magnolias have bright green leaves and large white fragrant flowers. The trees are usually planted for their beauty rather than for use.

Mangrove

Sea Turtle

Southern Magnolia

Shown here is a replica, or reproduction, of the inside of a Calusa chief's hut. The Calusa people lived in Southern Florida.

From the Beginning

The history of Florida is one of many people from different nations seeking a better life in a land they saw as golden. Florida is sometimes called "the state where everybody is from somewhere else." But all these people—native and new—are an important part of the state's history.

The First Floridians

No one really knows when the first humans arrived in today's Florida. But many experts think that Native Americans first reached the peninsula about 12,000 years ago. They believe that some of them might have come from present-day Central and South America, crossing the water into what is now the southern part of the state. Other Native Americans might have come from the northwestern part of today's United States. These natives might have walked across the icy land bridge that used to exist between Asia and North America.

Some large, dirt-covered mounds built by early Native Americans exist in the state today. They are called burial mounds. In many cases, the mounds contain human remains, religious artifacts, pottery, and jewelry.

It is estimated that when Europeans first arrived in the early sixteenth century, more than 100,000 Native Americans lived in present-day Florida. The Calusa and Tequesta

This illustration shows Ponce de León searching for the fountain of youth in Florida.

tribes lived in the south. These natives were hunters and gatherers. They speared fish for food, and they hunted bears, deer, and alligators with bows and arrows and clubs. They killed these animals for food and for clothing. The Timucua people, who lived in today's central and northeastern part of the state, hunted animals and maintained farms. The Apalachee people, who lived in the northwest, were also hunters and farmers. Both groups farmed corn, beans, squash, and pumpkins.

The Europeans Arrive

The written history of Florida begins in 1513 with a search for the fountain of youth. Some people believed that drinking from this fountain could keep a person young. King

Ferdinand of Spain sent an explorer named Juan Ponce de León in search of this fountain in a land called Bimini. But Bimini did not exist. Instead, Ponce de León and his men landed on the northeast coast of what is now Florida. It was on the day of Pascua Florida (Feast of the Flowers), which is Spain's Eastertime celebration. The explorer named the land la Florida in honor of the feast.

Ponce de León explored la Florida and its surroundings before sailing to Puerto Rico. In 1521, the explorer returned with two hundred people, fifty horses, and many supplies. His idea was to colonize the land for Spain. But fights with Native Americans made this too difficult. Ponce de León was wounded in one of these fights and sailed to Cuba, where he died.

Despite this setback, explorers continued to come to the region. In 1539, another Spanish explorer, Hernando de Soto, journeyed to the area in search of silver and gold, landing along the shore of what is now called Tampa Bay. But no great treasure awaited Hernando de Soto and his men. After exploring the southeast for several years, de Soto died from a fever in 1542 in present-day Louisiana, and the rest of his expedition went to Mexico. In 1559, Tristán de Luna y Arellano led another Spanish expedition to colonize today's Florida. He established a settlement at Pensacola Bay, but it was abandoned within two years after a series of misfortunes including illness and lack of food.

Besides searching for treasure, new trade routes, and land to colonize, many Europeans came to the area to spread the Catholic religion. Priests came hoping to convert the natives. The Native Americans had their own religions, which were very different from Christianity. Many did not want to convert. They were often beaten or killed when they refused. Other natives willingly converted. Still others, afraid and overpowered by the Europeans, practiced Christianity because they had no other choice.

During this time, many Spanish ships filled with treasures sailed the seas off the coast of present-day Florida. Most of them were headed back to Spain. The ships could carry a crew of about two hundred men. The chests of gold and silver were kept under guard in a room on the lower deck of the ship. But before they could reach Europe, many of these ships sank to the bottom of the ocean. Divers have found remains of some sunken treasure ships, while other vessels remain lost in the waters off Florida.

Did You Know?

The name "Punta Gorda" means "fat point" in Spanish. The city was named this because a broad part of the land in Punta Gorda juts into Charlotte Harbor.

The Native People

Florida was one of the first places discovered by the Europeans, but many people were living there long before the Spanish first landed. Native American tribes including the Creek, Choctaw, Miccosukee, Calusa, and Timucua lived throughout the region. The Choctaw and the Creek lived in northwestern Florida, while the Timucua lived in northeastern and central Florida. There were several tribes in the south of the state, including the Calusa, Ais, Jeaga, and Tequesta. The variety of cultures from these different tribes is very important to the history of Florida.

The Native Americans of Florida lived off the land. Many tribes fished, hunted, and farmed. To fish, Native Americans made boats by hollowing out tree trunks. Some tribes were talented basket weavers, while others created moccasins and beaded dolls. A few tribes played a game called stickball, which was a lot like lacrosse. Many of the clothes across tribes were very similar—men wore breechcloths and women wore blouses and skirts.

When the Europeans came to Florida, the changes devastated the Native Americans who lived there. In the 1500s, there were between 100,000 to 200,000 Native Americans in the Florida area. But diseases and wars killed off many people, and by the 1700s, very few survived. The Timucua tribe actually went extinct, the last living tribe member dying in 1767. Another tribe, the Calusa, was very advanced, beating the Spaniards in battle, and creating canals and man-made islands. Unfortunately, they nearly all died of disease, and the few remaining tribes people disbanded.

In the 1700s, several tribes including the Creek, Miccosukee, Hitchiti, and Oconee decided to band together. These people formed the Seminole tribe. The Seminole moved to Florida from Alabama and Georgia to look for more land. They fought several wars against the Europeans, and later the United States. Originally they lived in the northern part of the state, but war with the United States pushed the Seminole tribe farther and farther south. Today, there are two federally recognized tribes in Florida: the Seminole and the Micosukee.

Spotlight on the Seminole

The Seminole are descendants of the Creek tribe. A group of Creek people moved south from Alabama and Georgia to look for new land and to escape conflict between tribes. They called themselves "Seminole," which means "runaway" or "wild one."

After a series of three wars between the Seminole (joined by escaped African American slaves) and the United States government, the Seminole population decreased

A Seminole village in the 1800s.

from around 5,000 in the 1820s to less than 300 in the 1850s. Today, several thousand Seminole people live in Florida.

Clans: Each Seminole born becomes a member of his or her mother's clan. Husbands then join their wives' clans. Each clan is named after an entity that shares the clan's traits. There are eight Seminole clans: Panther, Deer, Wind, Bear, Bigtown/Toad, Snake, Bird, and Otter.

Homes: The Seminole house was called a chickee. At first, the Seminole lived in log cabin-type homes. Because of conflict, though, it became necessary for them to have homes that were quick and easy to build, in case they needed to move. Chickees were made with wood frames and roofs made of palm leaves.

Clothing: Women generally wore long skirts and short blouses. Seminole women **adorned** themselves with jewelry made with glass beads. Young women wore as much jewelry as they could. Older women wore less. Seminole men wore long shirts, sometimes with leather belts, and wool **turbans** on their heads.

Transportation: The Seminole used canoes that were dug from cypress tree logs. They used these canoes to travel and to spear fish when hunting.

Fun Facts: Many places in Florida get their names from Seminole words. "Hialeah" (city) means "prairie." "Ocala" (city) means "spring," and "Okeechobee" (lake) means "big water."

The Spanish, led by Pedro Menéndez de Avilés, dedicated San Agustín (Saint Augustine) in 1565.

The Spanish were not the only Europeans interested in colonizing Florida. The French began explorations, trying to claim Florida for France. A French explorer named Jean Ribault traveled through the area in 1562. By 1564, the French had established Fort Caroline along the Saint Johns River, near present-day Jacksonville.

Spain did not want the French to gain control over Florida. Pedro Menéndez de Avilés was sent to Florida to remove the French and strengthen Spanish control over the land. In 1565, he established a settlement on the Atlantic coast called San Agustín (Saint Augustine). It was the first permanent European settlement in what would later become the United States. Menéndez de Avilés and his men killed most of the French settlers. They took Fort Caroline from the French and renamed it San Mateo.

The French fought back two years later, when Dominique de Gourgues recaptured San Mateo and **executed** the Spanish soldiers stationed there. But the Spanish continued to set up forts and Catholic missions all across the region of northern Florida.

The English were also interested in controlling Florida. In 1586, the English captain Sir Francis Drake looted and burned Saint Augustine, although Spain still controlled Florida and most of what is now the southeastern section of the United States. But the English wanted more land and gradually captured it from the Spanish.

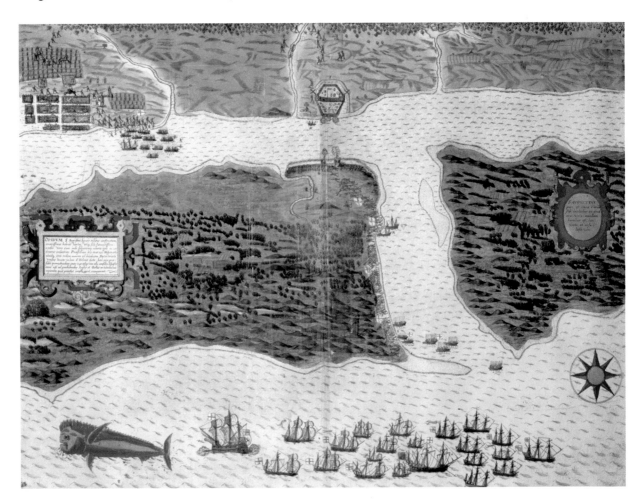

The 1586 destruction of Saint Augustine by the English fleet commanded by Sir Francis Drake.

Making Seashell Fish

There are thousands of species of saltwater fish in the waters surrounding Florida. Some of the kinds of fish that live there are grouper, flounder, snapper, and catfish. In a few easy steps, you can create your own fish!

What You Need

Assorted seashells
  (from the beach or a craft store)

Wiggly eyes in different sizes

Hot glue gun or instant glue

What To Do

- Lay out your shells. Use large shells for your fish's body. Use small shells as the dorsal fins, tail, and side fins.
- Once you have chosen your shells, glue the smaller shells onto the larger shells. If using a hot glue gun, have an adult help you.
- Glue wiggly eyes onto your fish.
- To display your fish, you can glue them to a piece of cardboard (such as a shoebox lid) and decorate it to look like the ocean!

Conflict and Changing Control

In 1702, English colonists in the Carolinas attacked Spanish Florida and again destroyed the town of Saint Augustine. But the Spanish fort there—Castillo de San Marcos—remained under Spain's control. The English colonists continued to take Spanish lands from Tallahassee to Saint Augustine. They destroyed Spanish missions and killed or took as slaves many Native Americans. The French, from their colony in Louisiana, pushed against Spanish Florida's western border and captured Pensacola in 1719, 21 years after the town had been established. After years of attacks from the British and French, Spain's power in the region had weakened. The British continued to move southward. By 1733, Georgia, which bordered Spanish Florida, was the southernmost British colony. Colonists living in Georgia continued to extend the colony's borders and fight the Spanish in Florida.

During the mid–1700s, Britain and France fought each other in North America in a conflict called the French and Indian War. Spain sided with the French during some of the fighting. When the war ended with a British victory in 1763, France lost almost all its land in eastern North America. The British took control of this land. During the war, the British had captured Havana on the island of Cuba, which had been controlled by Spain. Spain traded Florida to Britain in order to get back Havana. The British now controlled Florida.

Spanish soldiers at Castillo de San Marcos, their fort in Saint Augustine, fire cannons to repel a British attack.

The Battle of Pensacola, shown here, took place during the War of 1812. The U.S. fought against the Spanish and British. By the end of the battle, the British left, and the Spanish surrendered.

Do You Believe?

The Fountain of Youth Archaeological Park, in St. Augustine, is located on what many believe to be Ponce de León's landing site. The park is also home to a natural spring that some claim is the fountain of youth he was searching for. Today, visitors can drink from it!

Britain split Florida into two colonies. East Florida's capital was Saint Augustine, and Pensacola was the capital of West Florida. British control of the two Floridas lasted until Spanish troops marched back into West Florida during the American Revolution, which lasted from 1775 to 1783. The British surrendered parts of Florida to Spain in 1781. After they lost the war, the British gave up all of Florida to Spain. In 1783, Spain was once again in control of Florida.

But the end of the American Revolution was not an end to war in the region. Much of Florida still saw fighting. After the Revolution, Britain continued to encourage Native Americans, including the Seminoles and Creeks, to fight against American settlers. The British provided the natives with supplies and weapons to aid in these fights. The War of 1812, a result of unresolved problems between the United States and Britain, also brought unrest to the area.

Shown here is Saint Augustine under Spanish control.

10 KEY CITIES ★ ★ ★

Miami

Tampa

St. Petersburg

1. Jacksonville: population 821,784

At 840 square miles (2,176 sq km), Jacksonville is the largest city by landmass in the continental United States. Nicknamed "The River City," the St. Johns River flows right through the city. There are also many beaches, parks, and museums.

2. Miami: population 399,457

This vibrant city in Southern Florida is known for its dynamic culture. Shopping, fishing, nightlife, art, and architecture are just some of the things residents and visitors enjoy. Miami is also the largest U.S. city with a Spanish-speaking majority.

3. Tampa: population 335,709

Located on the west coast of Florida near the Gulf of Mexico, Tampa is a city that is growing fast. Thanks to a strong economy, outdoor activities, and major sports teams, Tampa is one of the most popular places to live in the Southeast.

4. St. Petersburg: population 244,769

St. Petersburg sits on a peninsula between the Gulf of Mexico and Tampa Bay. It is nicknamed "The Sunshine City," as it averages around 360 sunny days a year. St. Petersburg has also become a popular retirement city for senior citizens.

5. Orlando: population 238,300

Orlando is one of the most popular tourist destinations in the United States. It is home to many theme parks, including Walt Disney World, Universal Studios, and SeaWorld. The city is called "The Theme Park Capital of the World."

6. Hialeah: population 224,669

Hialeah, located northeast of Miami, has the highest percentage (74 percent) of Cuban and Cuban American residents in the United States. Around 90 percent of its residents speak Spanish fluently.

7. Tallahassee: population 181,376

Tallahassee, the capital of Florida and the largest city on Florida's panhandle, is a center for trade and agriculture. Two popular colleges, Florida State University and Florida A&M, are located in Tallahassee as well.

8. Fort Lauderdale: population 165,521

Fort Lauderdale is named for several forts that the United States built during the Second Seminole War in 1838. They were named after Major William Lauderdale. Today, the city is known for its many waterways, and it is often called the "Venice of America."

9. Port St. Lucie: population 164,603

Port St. Lucie is a popular destination for golfers. The Professional Golfers' Association (PGA) Village includes 54 holes of golf, a golf museum, and a learning center. The city is also home to the NY Mets' spring training camp.

10. Pembroke Pines: population 154,750

Located between Fort Lauderdale and Miami, Pembroke Pines is a residential city popular with commuters who want a quieter life. In 2010, *BusinessWeek* magazine named it one of the best places in Florida to raise children.

Tallahassee

Fort Lauderdale

Port St. Lucie

Seminoles prepare to attack American soldiers during the First Seminole War.

Some Americans in the Southern states, whose economies depended on African-American slave labor, were not pleased with Spanish control of Florida because slaves could flee across the border to freedom there. Many of these escaped slaves joined with the Seminoles. Americans in Georgia especially, as well as the federal government, were interested in making Florida part of the United States. Spanish control over Florida was weak, so U.S. troops continued to push into Florida, **engaging** in fighting against Native Americans and

African Americans there. This fighting escalated into the First Seminole War (1817–1818). During this war, U.S. general Andrew Jackson commanded the troops that fought the Seminoles and African Americans and captured major Spanish settlements. Under an 1819 treaty, Spain agreed to give Florida to the United States. It officially became part of the United States in 1821, and Andrew Jackson served as the territorial governor for a few months.

From Territory to State

After Florida became a territory, the two Floridas were combined, with Tallahassee as the new capital. Established in 1824, the city was chosen because it was halfway between the former capitals of Saint Augustine and Pensacola.

But peace did not come to Florida. As more and more people moved to the new territory, the white settlers decided they wanted Native American land. They also wanted escaped slaves removed from their Florida lands. In 1835, the Second Seminole War broke out between the U.S. government and the Seminole people, who did not want to leave their homeland and relocate west of the Mississippi River. By that time, Andrew Jackson was the president of the United States. The war ended in 1842, and the Seminoles were forced off their land. Some Seminoles left voluntarily, and some were captured and sent to reservations in the West. But others escaped and made new lives in Florida's Everglades.

In 1845, Florida became the twenty-seventh state. By 1850, the state's population had reached 87,445. In 1855, Florida's legislature passed the Internal Improvement Act.

The Second Seminole War broke out in 1835 when the Seminole people resisted the U.S. government's attempt to relocate them.

A group of slaves sits outside a house in St. Augustine in the mid-1800s.

Public land was offered to people who wanted to build businesses in Florida. Some transportation-industry businesses moved to Florida because of this act. The Third Seminole War (1855–1858) resulted in the forced relocation of more Seminoles to the West.

The Civil War

From the time the British first established colonies in North America, Southern **plantation** owners relied on African-American slaves to work their fields. To many white Southerners, this was their way of life. Without slaves, crops could not be grown, sold, or traded, and white landowners in the South would suffer. Florida had many of these plantations.

The Northern way of life was different. The North's economy did not depend on large plantations. Some antislavery states in the North thought that the slave states in the South were too powerful. Many Northerners also felt that slavery was morally wrong. These two issues helped lead to the Civil War.

Most Florida voters were not against slavery. When Abraham Lincoln ran for president in 1860, many Floridians disagreed with his politics, especially his antislavery position.

Lincoln won the election. On January 10, 1861, Florida seceded, or withdrew, from the Union (another name for the United States at the time). Florida was one of the eleven states that left the Union and joined together to form the Confederate States of America, leading to the Civil War.

Though very few Civil War battles were fought on Florida soil, Union forces occupied many of the coastal towns and forts. The interior of the state remained in Confederate hands, however.

Florida provided about 15,000 troops to the Confederate war effort, although more than 2,000 Floridians fought for the North. The state also provided many supplies, including salt, beef, pork, and cotton, to the Confederate army. In the end, the South was defeated, and Union troops took over the capital city of Tallahassee on May 10, 1865. Florida was once again part of the United States, though it was not officially readmitted to the Union as a state until 1868.

Confederate soldiers, wearing assorted uniforms, pose for a photograph in 1861 at Pensacola's Warrington Navy Yard.

The Miami area was devastated by the 1926 hurricane, which damaged fruit trees, homes, and businesses. The devastation marked the end of the Florida land boom.

Rebuilding and Growth

After so many years of fighting, Florida and other Southern states were in bad shape. The war had damaged their economies, and relations between Southerners and Northerners were poor. African Americans in the state still faced many problems. Many white people did not want to treat black people equally. After the Civil War, the federal government passed laws to protect the rights of black people. At the end of 1865, the Thirteenth Amendment to the U.S. Constitution, abolishing slavery in the United States, was ratified. With help from the federal government, Southern states set up new state governments, rejoined the Union, and began to restore their economies. Slowly, the Southern states were rebuilt.

During the late nineteenth century, Florida's economy grew stronger. Cattle raising became an important industry, as did growing citrus fruits such as oranges, grapefruits, and lemons. The Florida orange was becoming famous. The growth of these industries throughout the state prompted the construction of many roads and railroads.

By the early 1900s, Florida's population and wealth were increasing. The invention and popularity of automobiles made it even easier for people to travel to Florida. Many stayed on and contributed to the state's growth. But the good times did not last.

Hard Times and Wars

World War I lasted from 1914 to 1918. In 1917, the United States entered the war, joining several other countries—including France, Great Britain, Russia, and Italy—to fight against Germany, Austria-Hungary, Turkey, and Bulgaria. Florida provided supplies to the war effort. Many Floridians served in the military at this time.

The 1920s were difficult for Florida. Powerful hurricanes hit the state in 1926 and 1928. These storms killed so many fruit trees and destroyed so many homes and businesses that Florida's economy was badly hurt. Then, in 1929, Mediterranean fruit flies invaded many parts of the state, destroying crops. The citrus business was hit hard. Army troops set up roadblocks to stop people from bringing more infected fruit into the state. Florida's citrus production was reduced by more than half.

That same year, the entire country saw the beginning of what came to be called the Great Depression. Banks closed, and many businesses failed. Workers lost their jobs, and many families did not have enough money for food. People stopped traveling, and Florida's railroad companies were hurt. Florida was already experiencing hard times. The Great Depression, which lasted for about ten years, made the situation even worse.

After Japanese warplanes bombed the U.S. naval base at Pearl Harbor, Hawaii, in 1941, the United States entered World War II, joining the fighting against the governments of Germany, Japan, and Italy. World War II, which had begun in Europe in 1939, lasted until 1945. Once again, Florida provided necessary supplies for the troops. As in World War I, Floridians served in the military. Because of its warm climate, Florida became a major training center for U.S. soldiers, sailors, and pilots. More highways and airports were built to accommodate the increased traffic. These roads and airports became useful after the war, helping Florida's economy to grow.

Growth and Prosperity

Florida has experienced enormous population growth since World War II. Once one of the least populated and developed states in the nation, Florida became, by the early twenty-first century, the South's most populous state and the fourth most populous in the country. The growth occurred because Florida had a desirable climate and inexpensive land. The southern state was seen as a welcoming place.

Disney characters and park staff gather in front of Cinderella's Castle, shortly before the opening of Walt Disney World in 1971.

Throughout the state's history, tourism has always played an important role. But in the last part of the twentieth century, Florida tourism boomed. Thanks in large part to the opening of Walt Disney World, near Orlando, in 1971, Florida became the family vacation hot spot of the world. Visitors came for the theme parks as well as Florida's sunny beaches. Tourists wanted to see unique natural sites such as the Everglades and the Florida Keys. Through the years, many people have come to explore the islands, swim in the warm waters, see the coral reefs, and take part in the offshore fishing.

The citrus and fishing industries continued to bring money into the state. Mining and the new space and military technology industries also contributed to Florida's newfound **prosperity**. More businesses provided thousands of jobs.

Like other states, Florida was severely affected by the bad economic times that hit the country hard beginning in 2008. Many workers lost their jobs, some people could not afford to stay in their homes, and the tourist industry was hurt as fewer Americans had money to travel. Financial help from the federal government helped Florida's government and people cope with these problems as they looked forward to renewed economic growth and prosperity.

★ 10 KEY ★ DATES IN STATE HISTORY

1. April, 1513

After the King of Spain sent him to find a fountain of youth, Spanish explorer Juan Ponce de León lands on the northeast coast of present-day Florida. He claims the land for Spain.

2. September, 1565

After learning the French have explored and colonized Florida, Spain sends Pedro Menéndez de Avilés to drive them out. After coming ashore in September 1565, Menéndez de Avilés establishes San Agustín (Saint Augustine).

3. 1819-1821

In 1819, Spain gives up power over the Florida Territory to the United States in the Adams-Onis Treaty. It becomes effective in 1821.

4. March 3, 1845

Florida becomes the 27th state. By 1850 the population grows to more than 80,000, including more than 30,000 African-American slaves.

5. January 10, 1861

Residents in Florida believe the state, instead of the national government, should have the right to make its own laws. In January, Florida secedes, or withdraws, from the Union. The Civil War follows.

6. June 25, 1868

Florida is readmitted to the Union as a state. This is during a period of time called Reconstruction, when the government worked toward restoring the country after the war.

7. 1941-1945

Florida is a major training center for U.S. soldiers, sailors, and pilots during World War II. More than 200,000 Floridians serve in the military during the war.

8. January 28, 1986

The space shuttle *Challenger* explodes 73 seconds after launch from Cape Canaveral, killing all seven crew members. The crew included Christa McAuliffe, who was going to be the first teacher in space.

9. June 20, 2006

Dwyane Wade leads the Miami Heat to its first NBA Final win against the Dallas Mavericks. The team wins two more titles in 2012 and 2013.

10. February 26, 2012

The shooting death of an unarmed teenager, Trayvon Martin, in Sanford and the acquittal of his shooter in July 2013 spark protests across the United States.

Young Floridians enjoy the beach.

The People

The Sunshine State is home to more than 18 million people. Florida is the fourth-most-populous state in the nation, behind California, Texas, and New York. The state's population has also grown rapidly in recent decades, as people from other states and also from other countries have moved to the Sunshine State in large numbers. Florida's population has almost doubled just since 1980. As recently as 1960, fewer than 5 million people lived in Florida.

According to the 2010 U.S. Census, the population of Florida was 75 percent white, 16 percent African American, and 2.4 percent Asian American. About 22.5 percent was Hispanic (Hispanics may be of any race). Reflecting the fact that many people from other states choose to retire in Florida, the state has the highest percentage of people age 65 and older. Today, Floridians share their cultures, traditions, and opinions to make Florida such a diverse state.

Native Floridians

The original Native Americans of Florida, including the Timucua, Calusa, Apalachee, and Tequesta tribes, were killed by disease or warfare, were captured as slaves, or were forced to leave Florida by the Spaniards. The Seminole people, descendants of many

The Seminoles hold festivals all over Florida. This boy competes in an archery contest.

Native American tribes, had first come to Florida in the 1700s in search of new places to build homes. By the 1850s, when the United States declared an end to conflicts with the Seminoles, thousands of these Natives had been moved to reservations in the western United States. Some Seminoles remained in Florida by living in the swamps where U.S. soldiers and settlers could not find them. Most of today's Seminoles are the descendants of these Natives. Today, the state has six Seminole reservations, where several thousand Natives live.

Gatorade

In 1965, a University of Florida football coach wanted to find a way to help his team, the Gators. Players were affected by the heat during games. He spoke to physicians, who created a drink to replace components being lost through sweat. They called the beverage Gatorade.

The Seminoles have developed a strong economy to support their way of life. Tourism is one way Seminoles earn money. The Seminoles have a cultural museum as well as other tourist attractions, such as **ecotours** of the Florida Everglades. Visitors come to the reservations to enjoy these sites and learn more about the Seminole culture. Tourists also visit the reservations' casinos. Many Seminoles make a successful living in the citrus and cattle industries. The money that comes from tourism and agriculture helps pay for Seminole schools and health care.

The Seminoles also try to keep their traditions alive. They design some buildings like their ancestors' palm-thatched homes called chickees, although they do not live in them anymore. Many Seminoles wear colorful patchwork clothing of the past. Storytelling is an important part of the culture, and Seminole legends are passed down from old to young. The Seminoles are eager to share their history and culture with others. Some Seminoles visit schools in different parts of Florida to teach students about their traditions and their long history in the state. Seminoles also share their culture at the state's many Native American festivals.

This statue of Seminole chief Osceola is a symbol for Florida State University in Tallahassee.

Marjory Stoneman Douglas

Chris Evert

Ariana Grande

1. Ray Charles

Ray Charles was raised in Greenville, Florida. By age seven, Charles was completely blind, but he learned to play the piano. He played jazz, soul, gospel, and blues. Charles, who died in 2004, is respected for his successes over disability and racism as well as his contributions to music.

2. Marjory Stoneman Douglas

Marjory Stoneman Douglas, born in Minnesota in 1890, moved to Miami in 1915. A respected writer who fought for women's rights, racial equality, and environmentalism, Douglas is most famous for her dedication to preserving the Everglades.

3. Chris Evert

Born in Fort Lauderdale in 1954, Chris Evert began taking tennis lessons when she was five. She became the youngest player to reach the semifinals of the U.S. Open in 1971. Evert won 18 Grand Slam singles titles, and she was the number one player in the world for seven years.

4. Ariana Grande

Actress and singer Ariana Grande is the star of *Victorious* and *Sam & Cat* on Nickelodeon. Her debut album, *Yours Truly*, was released in 2013. Grande was born in Boca Raton, where she attended prep school and participated in theater.

5. Zora Neale Hurston

Born in Alabama, Hurston and her family moved to Eatonville, Florida when she was three. Hurston put herself through college, after which she became a writer. Her novel, *Their Eyes Were Watching God*, is considered one of the best novels written by an African American.

6. Enrique Iglesias

Enrique Iglesias was born in Spain in 1975 but moved to Miami in 1982. Enrique's interest in music began when he was in school. His 1995 debut album won a Grammy Award. He has since released numerous albums, selling millions of copies.

7. Osceola

Osceola was a Seminole leader who led successful battles against the U.S. during the Second Seminole War. When Osceola met Americans for peace negotiations in 1837, he was imprisoned. He died a year later.

8. Sidney Poitier

Sidney Poitier was born in Miami in 1927. As a teenager, he moved to New York City, where he joined a theater group. After acting in several films, Poitier became the first African American to win the Academy Award for Best Actor for his role in *Lilies of the Field* in 1963.

9. John Ringling

John Ringling helped found the Ringling Brothers Circus in 1884. In the 1920s, Ringling and his wife bought land in Sarasota, which became the circus' winter home. They also built a building to hold their art collection. This is now the John and Mable Ringling Museum of Art.

10. Tim Tebow

Born in the Philippines, Tim Tebow grew up in Florida. Tebow played quarterback at the University of Florida. He won the Heisman Trophy, an annual award to the top college football player, in 2007. Tebow later played for the Denver Broncos, New York Jets, and the New England Patriots.

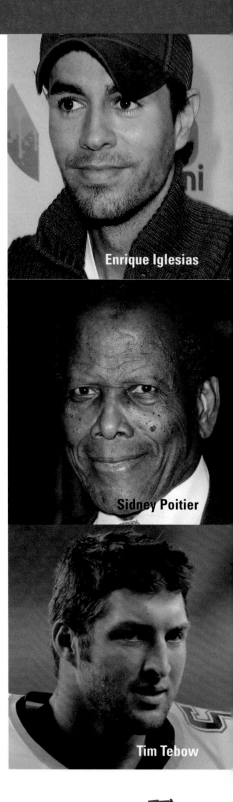

Enrique Iglesias

Sidney Poitier

Tim Tebow

Who Floridians Are

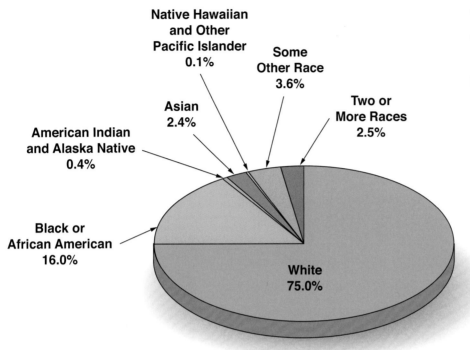

Native Hawaiian and Other Pacific Islander 0.1%

Some Other Race 3.6%

Asian 2.4%

Two or More Races 2.5%

American Indian and Alaska Native 0.4%

Black or African American 16.0%

White 75.0%

Total Population 18,801,310

Hispanic or Latino (of any race):
• 4,223,806 people (22.5%)

Note: The pie chart shows the racial breakdown of the state's population based on the categories used by the U.S. Bureau of the Census. The Census Bureau reports information for Hispanics or Latinos separately, since they may be of any race. Percentages in the pie chart may not add to 100 because of rounding.

Source: U.S. Bureau of the Census, 2010 Census

Cuban Americans

About 81 percent of Floridians were born in the United States. Of those born outside the United States, around 23 percent came from the neighboring island of Cuba. Since 1959, when Fidel Castro came to power and established a Communist government in Cuba, many Cubans have come to the United States to enjoy freedoms and economic opportunities not available in their own country. At certain times, the U.S. government has welcomed Cuban refugees, but at other times, U.S. government policy has made it difficult for Cubans to enter the country legally. The Cuban government has generally not allowed people to leave Cuba legally. Over the years, many Cubans have left their country secretly, traveling to south Florida on small, tightly packed boats or rafts. Crossing the water to Florida's shores is dangerous, and not all passengers have survived the journey.

In 1980, Castro's government let about 125,000 Cubans leave the country. Many traveled to the Miami area in small boats, some of which were provided by Cuban Americans. This event became known as the Mariel boatlift, because the refugees left from that Cuban port. Since a small number of the refugees had been released from Cuban jails, some Floridians at first did not trust the new arrivals. They worried that they would not know the difference between criminals and law-abiding Cubans. This tension made it more difficult for many of the Cubans to find jobs and acceptance.

Today, the Cuban-American community in Florida is a thriving community of well over one million people that plays a major role in the state's economy, cultural life, and politics. A number of Cuban Americans have been elected to the U.S. Congress. The largest concentration of Cuban Americans is in the Miami area. In fact, a part of Miami is called Little Havana, named after Cuba's capital city. Relations between the United States and Cuba have recently improved somewhat. In 2009, President Barack Obama lifted travel restrictions to Cuba for Cuban Americans. The changes made it easier for Cuban Americans to visit and also to send money to family members who are still living in Cuba.

People from Elsewhere in the Americas

Cubans are far from the only group of **immigrants** to Florida from the Caribbean and Latin America. As of 2011, 7.8 percent of Florida's population was born in Mexico, 4.6 percent came from Jamaica, and 5 percent from Haiti, which is one of the poorest countries in the world. In recent decades, many thousands of Haitians have tried to leave the country to find opportunity elsewhere. Many of these people have set out in small, overcrowded boats to reach the coast of south Florida. Some die at sea trying to make the trip.

This Cuban family in Florida enjoys dining at a Cuban restaurant.

More than 1,000,000 people from around the world visit Little Havana each year for the Calle Ocho street festival.

African Americans in Florida

Florida is home to many African Americans. Some black Floridians have come from other states or countries. Others have lived in Florida for generations.

A community, later known as Overtown, was set up in the northwestern section of Miami in 1896. At that time, laws in the South forced black people and white people to live separately. African Americans who worked in Miami lived in this part of town. Some of them worked in hotels, on the railroads, or in other businesses in Miami. Over the years, their hard work helped develop Miami and surrounding areas. African Americans in Overtown were proud of their community. They had schools, businesses, and churches. In the 1960s, laws outlawing segregation were passed. Many people who were living in Overtown chose to leave, but some stayed. Today, efforts are being made to revitalize Overtown and to remind people of its successes and historical importance.

From Near and Far

Floridians come from all different walks of life. A large portion of the population has relocated from other states, including many people who have chosen to retire in Florida. Retirement homes and communities in Florida are very popular. Many retirees come to the state to enjoy the weather and relax. They may be from different ethnic and economic backgrounds. What they have in common is an appreciation for the Sunshine State.

The Important Issue of Education

Education is an important issue for many Floridians. Florida's education system has seen great improvements since the late 1990s. The high school graduation rate for the 2011–2012 school year was 74.5 percent. Reading and math scores have been on the rise. Many attribute Florida's success to the A+ Plan. One part of the plan helps identify schools with underperforming students. These schools get money to improve resources to help students perform at grade level. Another feature of the plan rewards teachers whose students show marked improvements on statewide tests. The goal is to make sure that all of Florida's students have the chance to **excel**. In 2008, the U.S. Department of Education selected Florida to participate in the differentiated accountability pilot project. This program helps the state provide assistance to schools that need it most.

Florida has a vast college and university system. The State University System includes 12 schools around the state. Florida also has dozens of private colleges, universities, and community colleges.

The Florida State University Seminole football team prepares to play as their mascots, Osceola and his horse Renegade, ride by.

Daytona 500

Orange Bowl

Florida State Fair

1. Biketoberfest in Daytona Beach

This October festival celebrates everything motorcycles. More than 75,000 people from North America and Europe come to Daytona to look at old and new motorcycles, enjoy concerts, attend seminars, and participate in charity rides.

2. Daytona 500

Daytona Beach is famous for this annual February event. Tickets to watch the stock car races are often sold out a year in advance. The races, which originally took place on the beach, are now held at the Daytona International Speedway.

3. Discover Orange Bowl

The Orange Bowl is a college football game that is held every year around New Year's Day in Miami Gardens. It is one of the oldest Bowl games in the country.

4. Florida International Air Show in Punta Gorda

Military jets, aircraft exhibits, displays, and rides are just some of the things airplane enthusiasts see at this popular air show. The highlight of the show is watching pilots perform death-defying stunts in the air.

5. Florida State Fair in Tampa

Agricultural and **equestrian** events are the focal point of this annual state fair in February. Carnival rides, lots of good food, famous performers, exhibits, and even clowns attract people from all over the state.

FLORIDA ★ ★ ★ ★ ★

6. Miami International Boat Show

Nicknamed "The Greatest Boat Show in the World," this show features 2,000 exhibitors, 3,000 boats, and entertainment for five days in February.

7. St. Augustine's Birthday Celebration

On Labor Day weekend, the Spanish landing of 1565 is reenacted at the shoreline where the first settlers stepped off their ships. There is also a feast, which features a cooking contest, a birthday-cake cutting, and concerts.

8. Swamp Cabbage Festival

During the last full weekend in February, the town of LaBelle hosts this festival, named for the Florida state tree: the sabal, or cabbage, palm. This annual event features a rodeo, a parade, armadillo races, and food made from the sabal palm tree.

9. Wausau Possum Festival & Funday

In August, the town of Wausau honors the opossum, known locally as the possum, with activities such as a 5-kilometer (3.1-mile) race, a parade, and cornbread baking. There is even possum ice cream and possum stew!

10. Weeki Wachee Swamp Fest

In March, this annual festival is held on the banks of the Weeki Wachee River. This family-oriented event includes arts-and-crafts booths, music and dance performances, and a swamp monster costume contest.

Miami International Boat Show

St. Augustine Celebration

The Florida State Capitol building is located in Tallahassee.

How the Government Works

The state government of Florida is organized into three branches. The executive branch is headed by the governor. The legislative branch makes the state's laws, and the judicial branch includes the state's courts.

Each town or city in Florida has its own local government, run by a mayor, selectmen, or a **council** of officials. Voters in the towns and cities elect their local government officials. Each town or city belongs to a county. The counties are made up of several towns or cities. Often, there are governmental positions for the counties.

In 1968, Florida adopted a new state constitution. The legislature can propose changes, or amendments, to this constitution. Three-fifths of each legislative house must approve the proposed amendment. Citizens may also propose amendments by presenting a petition signed by a certain number of voters. For an amendment to be adopted, it must be approved by a majority vote of the people in an election.

The state government of Florida has also created special districts with governmental rights. These districts are not necessarily towns or cities. But it is important for these special districts to have a say in, and some control over, what occurs within them. For example, a special district was approved for Walt Disney World during the 1960s. This allows the Disney company to oversee the drainage of land in its area.

Every year, almost 250 middle and high school students work in Florida's House of Representatives' page and messenger program.

Branches of Government

Executive

The governor is the chief executive of the state of Florida. He or she serves a four-year term and cannot serve more than two terms in a row. The governor is responsible for appointing the heads of many state government agencies and for appointing many of the state's judges. The governor also signs or rejects bills that may or may not become laws.

Legislative

Like most other states and the federal government, Florida's lawmakers are divided into two houses: the senate, with 40 members, and the House of Representatives, with 120 members. These legislators represent certain parts of the state. The residents of those districts elect these lawmakers. Senators serve four-year terms and representatives serve two-year terms. Members of the senate or the house of representatives must live in the district they represent and be at least 21 years old. They cannot hold office for more than eight years in a row.

Judicial

The Florida courts decide whether someone accused of a crime has broken the law as well as settling disputes between individuals or companies. Most cases start in a trial, or circuit, court. Decisions of trial courts can be appealed to one of Florida's five district courts. District court decisions can be appealed to the state's highest court, the Florida Supreme Court, whose seven justices are appointed to six-year terms by the governor.

Floridians make a difference by volunteering in many ways. This family is collecting trash on a beach.

The governor signs a bill into law.

How a Bill Becomes a Law

Every year, Florida's House of Representatives and senate meet to discuss the issues that are important to the people of the state. In recent years, those issues have included crime, education, the environment, and the economy. Legislators decide whether new laws should be created or old laws changed. Suggestions for new laws can come from the senate or the House of Representatives.

These suggestions are called bills. A committee discusses a proposed bill. Members of the committee can make changes to the bill, and the committee rejects or approves it. Once the committee has approved a bill, it goes to the entire house to review. Like the committee, the entire house can change the bill, and it then rejects or approves the bill.

Both houses must approve a bill before it can become a law. A bill passed in one house goes to the other house for review. Once both houses approve the bill, it goes to the governor, who can sign and approve the bill, or reject—or veto—it. If the governor approves the bill, it becomes a law. If the governor vetoes the bill, the state legislature can override the veto with a two-thirds' vote in both houses. If the governor takes no action, the bill becomes a law after 60 days.

Citizens of Florida make a difference. These residents are protesting in Miami.

Robert Martinez:
Governor of Florida, 1987-1991

Robert "Bob" Martinez was born in 1934 in Tampa, where he later went to college. In 1979, Martinez ran for mayor of Tampa. In 1987, he became the first Hispanic to be elected Governor of Florida. As Governor, Martinez was an advocate of laws and rules that protected waterways, manatees, and dolphins.

Janet Reno:
U.S. Attorney General, 1993-2001

Janet Reno was born in Miami in 1938. She attended Cornell University and then Harvard Law School. Reno practiced law in Florida until 1993, when President Bill Clinton appointed her Attorney General. The Attorney General represents the United States and gives legal advice to the government. Reno was the first woman ever to hold the position.

Marco Rubio: U.S. Senator, 2011-

Born in Miami in 1971, Marco Rubio is the son of Cuban immigrants. He attended the University of Florida and earned a law degree from the University of Miami. Rubio was elected to the West Miami City Commission in 1998 and then the Florida House of Representatives in 2000. In 2009, Rubio was elected U.S. Senator.

FLORIDA
YOU CAN MAKE A DIFFERENCE

What You Can Do

America has a long history of ordinary citizens making extraordinary changes. Although it often seems as if one person cannot make a difference, that is certainly not true. In Florida, the Governor's Points of Light Award is presented every week to volunteers in the state who are active in their community. Floridians of all ages have won this award.

Contacting Lawmakers

Floridians can contact members of the state legislature to make their views known. To get an email or mailing address for a state senator or representative, you can go to these websites:

http://www.myfloridahouse.gov/Sections/Representatives/representatives.aspx

http://www.flsenate.gov/Senators/Find

The Florida legislature has programs to get young people involved in government. The state House of Representatives has a page and messenger program, in which each representative sponsors one page (age 12 to 14) and one messenger (age 15 to 18) for a week. The state senate has a page program for students fifteen to eighteen years of age. The young people deliver messages, distribute materials, and even sit in on committee meetings.

But you do not need to join a government organization to make a difference in your state. You can help out at homeless centers, animal shelters, or assisted-living communities. You can work for a candidate running for political office or lend a hand at a food kitchen. There are hundreds of volunteer opportunities. You can also make sure you are aware of what is going on around your state. Try to listen to or read your local and state news. There might be issues about which you feel strongly. You can make a difference.

Scuba diving in the Gulf of Mexico and the Atlantic Ocean are popular activities in Florida.

Making a Living

Floridians earn a living in many different ways. The majority of state residents work in service industries, helping other people or businesses. Service workers in Florida include salesclerks, real estate agents who sell homes or other property, hotel desk clerks, food servers in restaurants, and even the people who wear Mickey Mouse costumes at Disney World. Since Florida is the vacation capital of the world, it is no wonder so many people work in service jobs. But the state's economy—all the goods people make, what they sell, and the services they provide to others—is more than just service jobs. Agriculture, manufacturing, and mining are also important parts of Florida's economy.

Tops in Tourism

Florida's economy relies heavily on tourism. Many Florida businesses depend on the money tourists spend. Many Florida workers provide goods and services to visitors. Also, the state government depends on tourism for a significant portion of the state's tax **revenue** because Florida has no state income tax. People who live and work in Florida do not have to give part of the money they earn (their income) to the state.

A statue of Walt Disney and Mickey Mouse stands in front of Cinderella's Castle at Walt Disney World.

The major way that the state collects money for government programs is through the state sales tax. The sales tax is added to goods and services sold in the state. The state collects this money from the companies that sell the goods and services. Florida residents pay a large part of the sales tax, of course. But if tourists did not come to the state to stay in hotels or campgrounds, eat in restaurants, shop in stores, and more, the state of Florida would collect less money to pay for government services.

The tourist industry brought $67 billion into the economy of Florida in 2011. In Florida's tourist industry, Disney is tops. Walt Disney World brings money and jobs into the state. Because of Disney's success, other theme parks have been built in the Orlando area. Hotels have sprung up there and elsewhere in the state to give the tourists a place to stay. Cruise ships dock in Florida ports every day, bringing many tourist dollars into the state.

Many tourists come to Florida to set sail on cruises to the Caribbean islands.

★ 10 KEY INDUSTRIES ★

Agriculture

Construction

Fishing

1. Aerospace

With more than 2,000 aerospace-related companies located there, Florida's aerospace industry ranks second in the United States. This industry employs more than 80,000 people. The John F. Kennedy Space Center manages and operates the country's space launches.

2. Agriculture

Florida produces 67% of the oranges eaten in the United States. The state's warm climate makes it the perfect place for citrus plants, including grapefruit and tangerines. Around 40% of the world's orange juice comes from Florida.

3. Construction

Florida is one of the fastest growing destinations for people who want to move to a different state. This growth means that there is a demand for new housing and businesses. Because of this growth, the construction industry is booming.

4. Education and University Research

Teachers are in demand because of increased population and annual teacher retirements, making education a top industry in the state. In addition, more than $500 million of sponsored research takes place in Florida's universities each year.

5. Fishing

The fishing industry in Florida brings in millions of dollars a year. Fishers make the most money from shrimp, lobsters, and scallops. Saltwater fish such as grouper, mackerel, and red snapper are also moneymakers. A popular freshwater fish is catfish.

6. Health Technology

Health technology is the business of using science to develop technology for healthcare. In recent years, this industry has experienced around a 20% growth.

7. Hospitality and Tourism

Ever since Walt Disney World opened, theme parks have been a key part of the state's tourism industry. The state has water parks, parks based on movie studios, wildlife parks, and amusement parks with games and rides. The popularity of these places keeps people coming to the state year after year.

8. Mining

Around 4/5 of the United States' phosphate rock, which is used in fertilizer, is produced in Florida. Other things that are mined in the state include oil and limestone.

9. Real Estate

Florida's population growth means people are buying more homes. Florida's real estate industry has been known to be rocky, but experts have said that the improving economy has helped the real estate business stabilize.

10. Sales and Retail

Florida is one of the top tourist destinations in the world. The state is also experiencing population growth, as many people are choosing Florida as their new home. The sales and retail industry is keeping up with this growth. Automotive and food sales are some of the biggest sectors.

Hospitality and Tourism

Real Estate

Sales and Retail

Recipe for Orange Oat Muffins

The state fruit isn't just for juice. Oranges can be used in many recipes, such as cookies, cakes, salads, and smoothies. With the help of an adult, follow this recipe to make delicious and healthy orange muffins!

What You Need

Zest of 2 oranges

1/2 cup (100 g) plus 2 tablespoons (30 g) sugar

1/3 cup (71 ml) canola oil

2 large eggs

1/2 teaspoon (2.5 ml) vanilla extract

1/3 cup (71 ml) plus 1 tablespoon (15 ml) orange juice

4 tablespoons (25 g) rolled oats, plus more for topping

1 1/2 cup (165 g) all-purpose flour

2 1/2 (12.5 g) teaspoons baking powder

Pinch of salt

What to Do

- Preheat oven to 375°F (191°C).
- Line a muffin pan with liners or lightly grease it with cooking spray or butter.
- In a large bowl, whisk together orange zest, sugar, oil, eggs, and vanilla until well combined, about 3 to 4 minutes.
- Stir in the orange juice and rolled oats.
- In a small bowl, mix together flour, baking powder, and salt.
- Fold this mixture into the wet ingredients. Do not over mix.
- Pour mixture into muffin pan, filling each hole 3/4 full.
- Sprinkle with rolled oats.
- Bake 20 to 25 minutes or until golden and a toothpick inserted in the center comes out clean.
- Let cool in the pan for 5 minutes before moving them to a wire rack.
- Serve warm or at room temperature.

Throughout the year, tourists take advantage of the state's warm weather and outdoor activities. Florida's beaches are very popular. Some people visit the Everglades to see the state's wildlife. The Florida Keys are also an appealing destination. The islands are ideal for snorkeling, diving, swimming, fishing, exploring the tropical wilderness, visiting historic sites, or enjoying the local events. Many tourists visit the Kennedy Space Center at Cape Canaveral to learn about space exploration.

Products from the Land

Tourism is not the only way people and companies in the state of Florida make money. Raising livestock is important, and while agriculture was the state's first major industry, it continues to be important today. Florida is the second-largest agricultural state in the southeast, after North Carolina. In 2011, agricultural **exports** were worth $4 billion.

The star of agriculture in Florida is the orange. Florida ranks first among all states in orange juice production. Farmers harvest peanuts and pecans in northern Florida. Cauliflower, broccoli, and sweet corn also grow in Florida. In February and March, boxcars filled with winter produce head north out of Florida. This produce includes snap beans, squash, celery, and tomatoes. These foods ship mostly to states where the winters are cold and the growing seasons are short.

Florida leads the nation in the sale of many major fruits and vegetables. Among other types of fruit, Florida farms grow oranges, grapefruits, mangoes, watermelons, tangerines, limes, and tangelos. Farmers also grow vegetables such as peppers, sweet corn, cucumbers, and beans. Because of year-round warm weather, the state also provides the rest of the country with houseplants, ferns, and flowers.

Ranches around the state breed cattle for the beef industry. Cows are raised on dairy farms, as well. Ranchers also raise hogs and poultry.

Florida is one of the leading suppliers of phosphate. Phosphate is mined in Florida and shipped to the rest of the country and around the world. Most phosphate is used to make plant fertilizers. Other products in which phosphate is used include food for farm animals.

An Atlas V rocket, carrying the *Maven* spacecraft, takes off from Cape Canaveral in November 2013. *Maven* is on a journey to the planet Mars.

Area Code 321

In 1999, the part of Florida that includes Cape Canaveral got a new area code: 321. This number was chosen because it is the end of a space-launch countdown [3-2-1 liftoff!].

Making Things

There are factories across Florida, although manufacturing plays a small role in the state's economy. At food-processing plants, many of the state's agricultural products, such as citrus fruits, are made into juices and jams. Paper mills also dot the state.

Companies in the state make equipment needed to run the space programs at Cape Canaveral. The state also has military and aerospace industries. New technology is developed at government labs. This technology is important for both space exploration and military defense.

Keeping a Balance

Florida's population and economy have grown tremendously in recent decades. This growth has led to the construction of many homes, businesses, schools, and highways. It has increased demand for such things as water and electricity as well as the amount of waste to be disposed of. These and other changes have put pressure on the state's environment and natural resources. An issue for Floridians today is how to strike the right balance between continuing the state's growth and protecting its environment.

One of Florida's great natural resources is its coral reefs. Florida is the only place in the United States with a long line of coral reefs in its coastal waters. Coral reefs are underwater formations made up of both living and nonliving elements. The base of a coral reef is limestone. Most of this limestone is the skeletons of dead corals (a type of marine animal). Living corals make up the top of the reef, closest to the surface of the water. Coral reefs provide shelter and food for many underwater plants and animals. They also protect the land from waves from the ocean. Many medicines are made from plants and animals living on or among coral reefs.

Every year, thousands of scuba divers and snorkelers—both tourists and state residents—visit Florida's coral reefs. Some touch or step on the living corals. Broken or scraped corals can become infected and die. Boaters and fishers also accidentally start these infections when they hit the corals. Corals also need clear, clean water to grow. Water pollution from factories, cities, and farms has become a problem in Florida.

The state government and the U.S. Coral Reef Task Force have tried to protect Florida's coral reefs. But they cannot do it alone. It is up to both residents and visitors to understand that in a matter of seconds they can destroy some of the rare beauty of a coral reef.

In 2013, a professor from Miami discovered that some coral reefs had the ability to activate a set of genes to make a protein that would help the coral acclimatize, or get used to, its environment. Since all types of coral share common genes, it may be possible to activate these genes in other species. More research and testing is needed, but this discovery gives us hope that coral reefs in Florida and around the world can be saved.

FLORIDA

STATE MAP

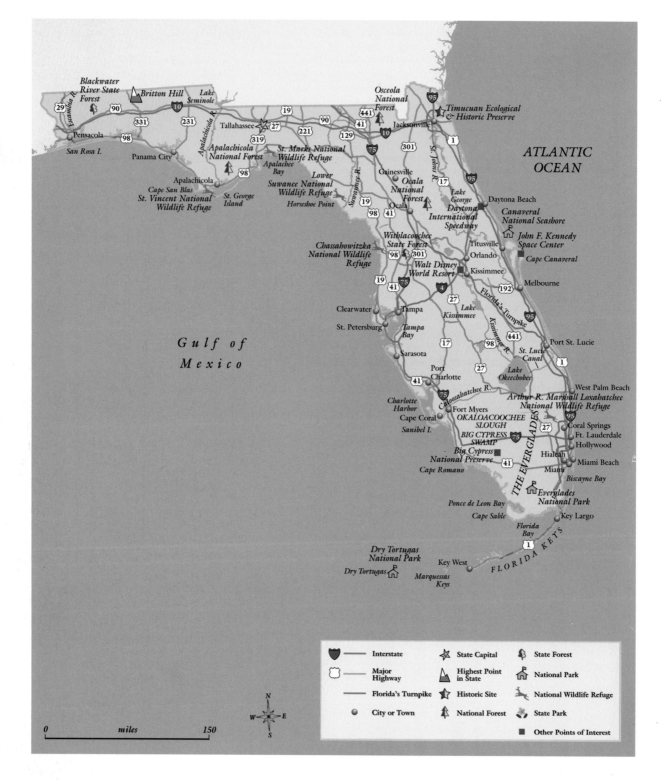

Blackwater River State Forest
Britton Hill
Lake Seminole
Escambia R.
Apalachicola R.
29
90
331
231
10
98
Pensacola
San Rosa I.
Panama City
Apalachicola
Cape San Blas
St. Vincent National Wildlife Refuge
St. George Island
Apalachicola National Forest
Apalachee Bay
Tallahassee
27
319
221
90
19
St. Marks National Wildlife Refuge
Lower Suwanee National Wildlife Refuge
Horseshoe Point
Suwanee R.
129
41
10
301
19
98
41
Gainesville
Ocala National Forest
Ocala
St. Johns R.
17
St. Johns R.
Lake George
Osceola National Forest
Jacksonville
1
Timucuan Ecological & Historic Preserve
ATLANTIC OCEAN
95
Daytona Beach
Daytona International Speedway
Canaveral National Seashore
John F. Kennedy Space Center
Cape Canaveral
Withlacoochee State Forest
Chassahowitzka National Wildlife Refuge
98
301
19
41
Walt Disney World Resort
Titusville
Orlando
Kissimmee
4
Melbourne
95
192
Florida's Turnpike
Clearwater
Tampa
St. Petersburg
Tampa Bay
27
Lake Kissimmee
Gulf of Mexico
Sarasota
17
Kissimmee R.
441
98
Port St. Lucie
St. Lucie Canal
1
Port Charlotte
41
27
Lake Okeechobee
West Palm Beach
Arthur R. Marshall Loxahatchee National Wildlife Refuge
Charlotte Harbor
Caloosahatchee R.
Fort Myers
Cape Coral
Sanibel I.
OKALOACOOCHEE SLOUGH
BIG CYPRESS SWAMP
Big Cypress National Preserve
Cape Romano
75
27
41
THE EVERGLADES
Coral Springs
Ft. Lauderdale
Hollywood
Hialeah
Miami Beach
Miami
Biscayne Bay
95
Everglades National Park
Ponce de Leon Bay
Cape Sable
Key Largo
Florida Bay
1
Dry Tortugas National Park
Dry Tortugas
Key West
Marquessas Keys
FLORIDA KEYS

0   miles   150

N
W   E
S

Interstate		State Capital		State Forest	
Major Highway		Highest Point in State		National Park	
Florida's Turnpike		Historic Site		National Wildlife Refuge	
City or Town		National Forest		State Park	
				Other Points of Interest	

FLORIDA ★ ★ ★ ★ ★
MAP SKILLS

1. **What is Florida's highest point?**

2. **What interstate runs along the eastern coast of Florida?**

3. **What is Florida's westernmost national wildlife refuge?**

4. **What river runs between Fort Meyers and Lake Okeechobee?**

5. **What national park is located on one of the Florida Keys?**

6. **What historic site is located outside Jacksonville?**

7. **What major highway takes you from Tampa to Miami?**

8. **What river connects Lake Seminole and the Gulf of Mexico?**

9. **To get from Walt Disney World Resort to Tampa, what route would you take?**

10. **What point of interest is located near Cape Canaveral?**

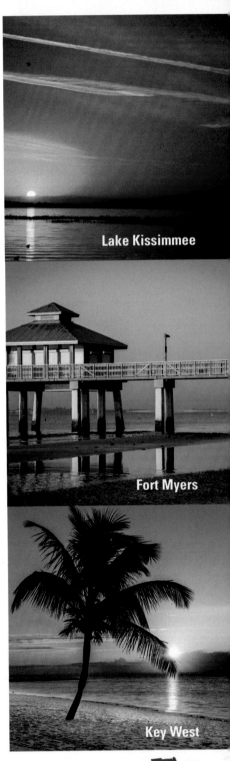

Lake Kissimmee

Fort Myers

Key West

1. Britton Hill
2. Interstate 95
3. St. Vincent National Wildlife Refuge
4. Caloosahatchee River
5. Dry Tortugas National Park
6. Timucuan Ecological Historic Preserve
7. 41
8. Apalachicola River
9. Interstate 4
10. John F. Kennedy Space Center

State Seal, Flag, and Song

The official seal shows rays of sunshine on the Florida coast. It shows a Seminole woman spreading flowers, a sabal palm, and a steamboat. At the bottom of the seal is the state's motto, "In God We Trust." Some aspects, such as the native dress, the steamboat design, and the tree were incorrectly drawn in the original version from 1868. The state adopted this corrected version in 1985.

Florida's flag is white with two bold red stripes that begin at each edge and form a large X. During the late 1890s, Governor Francis P. Fleming suggested that the cross be added so that the banner did not appear to be a white flag of truce or surrender when hanging. In the middle of the flag is Florida's state seal. This current version was adopted in 1900.

To see the lyrics of the Florida State Song, "The Swanee River," go to
www.statesymbolsusa.org/Florida/floridastatesong.html

Glossary

adorned	Enhanced the appearance of especially with beautiful objects.
council	A group of people who are chosen to make rules, laws, or decisions about something.
development	The act or process of growing or causing something to grow or become larger.
ecosystem	The complex of a community of organisms and its environment functioning as a unit.
ecotours	Tours of natural habitats in manners meant to reduce impact on nature.
engaging	Very attractive or pleasing in a way that holds your attention.
environment	The conditions and influences that affect the growth and health of someone or something.
equestrian	Of or relating to the riding of horses.
evaporate	To change from a liquid into a gas.
excel	To be better than others.
executed	Killed especially as punishment for a crime.
exports	Products that are sent to another country to be sold there.
immigrants	People who come to a country to live there.
launch	To send or shoot something into the air, water, or outer space.
plantation	A large area of land especially in a hot part of the world where crops (such as cotton) are grown.
prosperity	The state of being successful usually by making a lot of money.
revenue	Money that is made by or paid to a business or an organization.
thrives	Gains in wealth or possessions.
turbans	Head coverings that are worn especially by men that are made of long cloths wrapped around the head.

More About Florida

BOOKS

Bodden, Valerie. *Florida (Let's Explore America)*. Mankato, MN: Creative Education, 2011.

Furstinger, Nancy. *Everglades (Wonders of the World)*. New York, NY: Av2 by Weigl, 2013.

Jerome, Kate Boehm. *Orlando, FL: Cool Stuff Every Kid Should Know*. Mount Pleasant, SC: Arcadia Publishing, 2010.

Sammons, Sandra Wallus. *Ponce de Leon and the Discovery of Florida*. Sarasota, FL: Pineapple Press, 2013.

Suben, Eric. *The Spanish Missions of Florida*. New York, NY: Scholastic, 2010.

WEBSITES

Everglades National Park—For Kids:

www.nps.gov/ever/forkids/index.htm

Florida Kids Home Page:

dhr.dos.state.fl.us/kids

Florida's Official Website:

www.myflorida.com

Kennedy Space Center Attractions:

www.kennedyspacecenter.com/attractions.aspx

ABOUT THE AUTHORS

Debra Hess has created many different types of educational materials for children across America. She was also the editor of Scholastic Action Magazine, a publication for at-risk middle and high school students. Hess has been the Creative Director for Children's Content at a research division of AT&T, has written for an award-winning children's television series, and is the author of dozens of books for children.

Lori P. Wiesenfeld has spent most of her career in reference, children's, and educational publishing. She was the managing editor of The World Almanac and Book of Facts and The World Almanac for Kids. Before that, she was an editor for Funk & Wagnalls New Encyclopedia. She is currently a freelance editor, working on a wide variety of publications.

Index

Page numbers in **boldface** are illustrations.

Index